PET
Groomer

by Marie Pearson

raintree
a Capstone company — publishers for children

Raintree is an imprint of Capstone Global Library Limited, a company incorporated in England and Wales having its registered office at 264 Banbury Road, Oxford, OX2 7DY – Registered company number: 6695582

www.raintree.co.uk
myorders@raintree.co.uk

Editor: Mirella Miller
Designer: Becky Daum
Production Specialist: Ryan Gale

ISBN 978 1 4747 7477 2 (hardback)
ISBN 978 1 4747 8131 2 (paperback)

British Library Cataloguing in Publication Data
A full catalogue record for this book is available from the British Library

Acknowledgements
iStockphoto: 2002lubava1981, 6, andriano_cz, 8–9, Darunechka, 14–15, LuckyBusiness, 23, ollegN, 11, Ranta Images, 27, Thepalmer, 30–31; Shutterstock Images: A_Lesik, 26, Anton Gvozdikov, 12–13, Eric Isselee, 17, 28, Ligfo, 9, LightField Studios, cover, nazarovsergey, 20–21, Nomad_Soul, 19, rodimov, 24, sirtravelalot, 5, Susan Schmitz, 6–7, Tinxi, 16–17.

Every effort has been made to contact copyright holders of material reproduced in this book. Any omissions will be rectified in subsequent printings if notice is given to the publisher.

CONTENTS

PET Groomer

The groomer clips a dog's nails. She cleans its ears. She scrubs it with shampoo in a special bath tub. Then she rubs in conditioner.

The groomer lifts the dog to the drying table. She uses a blow dryer. It dries and loosens fur.

Groomers wash pets in special baths.

The groomer brings the dog to the grooming table. She brushes the dog. This helps it shed less. She shaves the fur between its paw pads. She trims its ear hair. The dog's bottom can also get shaved. This helps it stay clean.

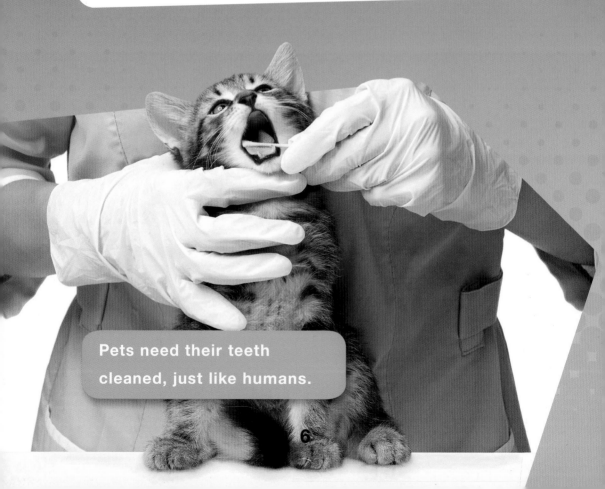

Pets need their teeth cleaned, just like humans.

6

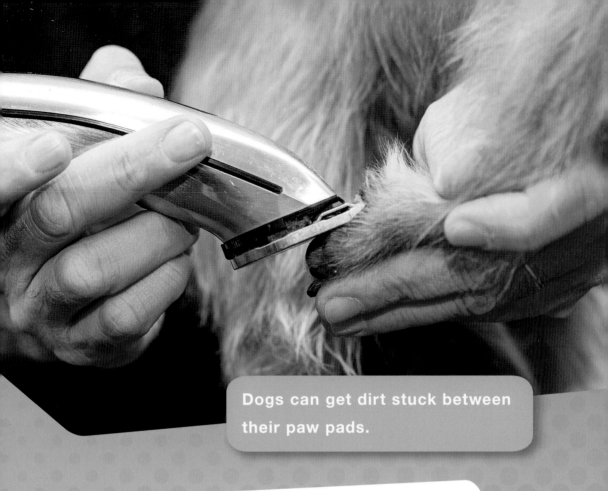

Dogs can get dirt stuck between their paw pads.

Groomers have many tasks. They brush teeth. They give full haircuts. They clip nails. They clean ears.

Groomers remove ticks from dogs' ears and fur.

Groomers usually groom dogs and cats. But they might also work with rabbits or other **species**. Some groomers work with only one species.

Groomers help keep pets healthy. They see every inch of a pet. They might find an ear **infection**. They might find a cut. They can tell owners if the pet needs a **vet** visit.

Rabbits sometimes need to get their nails clipped.

9

CHAPTER 2

QUALITIES AND
Skills

Groomers love animals. Many groomers work with all kinds of pets every day. They are confident around all pets.

Groomers are patient and kind.
Pets wriggle and shake. They can also
bite if they get scared. Being patient can
help to calm animals. Groomers are also
careful. They use sharp tools.

Not all pets enjoy getting baths. Groomers must be careful so they do not get scratched.

Groomers handle every part of dogs' thick coats.

A MESSY JOB

Groomers can handle gross things! Some dogs have poo in their bottoms. Others have eye gunk. The groomer has to clean them off. Sometimes there are bugs in a dog's thick coat.

STRENGTH NEEDED

Groomers need to be strong. They lift pets. Some dogs weigh more than 90 kilograms (200 pounds).

Groomers know how to care for all fur types. Some owners do not groom their pets enough. Cats may come in with long, **matted** fur. Groomers know how to safely shave off matted fur without cutting the animal.

WORKING WITH OWNERS

Groomers have good communication skills. They work with pet owners. They need to understand what owners want. Sometimes owners get upset. Groomers need to be calm and polite. They should be honest if they have made a mistake.

Groomers shave matted fur instead of cutting it out. This helps to stop the animal being injured.

Groomers sometimes use dog hair spray to keep a dog's fur fluffy and full.

Groomers know how to make pets look good. Different breeds of dogs get different haircuts. Good groomers know each one. They can do a full haircut or just a trim.

WHAT DO YOU THINK?

Some groomers compete in grooming competitions. They can even make dogs look like other animals. Do you think this is right?

Some owners want their pets to be colourful.

17

CHAPTER 3

THE
Workplace

Groomers are needed anywhere there are pets. They work in many places. Some work in grooming **salons**. These businesses specialize in grooming pets.

Others work at boarding kennels or vet clinics. Groomers might also work from home.

Grooming salons have all the tools groomers need to clean pets.

Groomers use many different tools in their work.

Some groomers travel to clients in a special van. The van has a bath and a water tank. It has everything groomers need to groom pets.

THE PAY

Groomers generally make about £8.50 per hour. Some get paid an annual **salary**. Some make a **percentage** of the cost of grooming. Groomers are often given **tips**.

BRUSHES

There is a different brush for every type of fur. Some brushes are only good for short fur. Pet groomers know when to use each type of brush.

CHAPTER 4

EDUCATION

Groomers do not need to go to college or university. But they should have experience handling animals. They should know animal **behaviour**. This helps them handle pets safely.

Apprentices might help groomers wash and dry pets.

GETTING EXPERIENCE

Groomers get experience in many ways. Some people take online courses. Others go to college. Students learn by handling real pets. They learn about different breeds. They learn how to care for all fur types.

Some students work as **apprentices**. They watch and help a groomer. The groomer teaches them the skills they need.

Pets leave the salon
looking their best.

A good groomer cares about pets. Owners will keep coming back to these groomers. Owners know their pets are in good hands. The pets will go home looking fabulous.

It is important to take care of your pet. They should be well groomed and cared for.

GLOSSARY

apprentice
person learning a job from someone already skilled in that job

behaviour
way in which a living being acts

infection
disease from bacteria

matted
tangled together tightly

percentage
portion of the full amount

salary
regular payment by an employer

salon
business that provides grooming services for pets

species
group of plants or animals of the same kind that can produce offspring together

tip
money given in addition to the cost of a service

vet
doctor who takes care of animals

OTHER JOBS TO CONSIDER

BOARDING KENNEL WORKER

Many dogs stay at a kennel when their owners are away. Boarding kennel workers take care of them. The workers feed the dogs and exercise them.

DOG WALKER

Some owners are not able to walk their dogs. They hire a dog walker. Dog walkers may walk many dogs at once. They help dogs get exercise.

PET SITTER

Some animals stay at home while their owners are away. The owners hire pet sitters to take care of them. Pet sitters go to people's homes. They feed and play with the pets.

ACTIVITY

WATCH, LEARN AND DO

Many pet shops have pet groomers. See if your local pet shop has this service. Go to the pet shop and ask the workers there if you can watch the groomers at work. What tasks do the groomers do? What pets do they work with?

If you have a pet, ask your parents about how it stays clean. Perhaps you can help give your dog a bath. Or if you have a cat, you could help brush your cat's fur.

FIND OUT MORE

Want to know more about pet grooming? Learn more here:

Books

Caring for Dogs and Puppies and *Caring for Cats and Kittens*, Ben Hubbard (Franklin Watts, 2015)

Pets' Guides series, Anita Ganeri, Isabel Thomas and Rick Peterson (Raintree, 2013–14)

Website:

City & Guilds: advice on what qualifications are needed to be a dog groomer www.cityandguilds.com/qualifications-and-apprenticeships/land-based-services/animal-management/7763-dog-grooming#tab=information

Note to reader: never attempt to groom your pet yourself. You may harm it. Animal grooming should always be done by a responsible adult.

INDEX